GNOME ROAD PUBLISHING
Louisville, Kentucky, USA
www.gnomeroadpublishing.com
Logo designs by Wendy Leach, copyright © 2023 by Gnome Road Publishing
Special thanks to Bonnie Kelso for cover and book design assistance.

Summary: A kid-friendly poetry collection with facts about colorful animals found
throughout the world and an introduction to simple and fun poetic forms.

Identifiers: ISBN 978-1-957655-04-8 (trade) | ISBN 978-1-957655-09-3 (ebook)

LC record available at: https://lccn.loc.gov/2022939023

The text of this book is set in Catseye and Le Monde Libre Cla Std fonts.

First Edition
10 9 8 7 6 5 4 3 2 1
Manufactured in India

Animals In Surprising Shades

Poems About Earth's Colorful Creatures

Written by Susan Johnston Taylor

Interior Illustrations by Annie Bakst

Animals in Surprising Shades

Ever seen a purple snail?

A spotted newt with orange tail?

If you'd like to take a look,

please turn the pages of this book.

For nature's full of brilliant hues,

vivid pinks to navy blues.

Come marvel at the painted bugs,

speckled frogs and ruffled slugs.

Poetic Form ~ An **octave** is an eight-lined poem. "Oct" means eight, like the eight limbs of an octopus. Some definitions require a specific meter and rhyme scheme, while others define an octave as any eight-lined poem, with or without rhyme.

Strawberry Poison Dart Frog

Juicy red like a four-legged fruit,
these fierce and flashy frogs all sport
stunning colors and patterns.
Still, predators beware!
Because although they
look delicious,
these frogs are
dressed to …
kill.

Poetic Form ~ A nonet is a nine-line poem that starts with a one-syllable or nine-syllable line. Then each line counts up or down in syllables, moving from 1 to 9 or 9 to 1.

Does the idea of strawberry frogs make you hungry?

Don't eat them! Poison dart frogs come in bright colors warning predators to stay away. This is a survival strategy called **aposematic coloration.** Are all species of poison dart frogs poisonous? No, but some are. Strawberry dart frogs get toxins from insects they eat. Their skin releases toxins when they feel threatened.

Can you regrow a lost arm or eye?

Newts can. Scientists hope studying how newts **regenerate** lost tissue will inspire discoveries for human medicine. Red-spotted eastern newts also change colors as they grow. They shift from yellowish-green to reddish-orange and move from water to land and back again.

Eastern Newt

Who's this tiny orange critter,
slithering across leaves,
hiding under rocks,
tail curving into a question mark?

That's an eastern newt!
And in time, he may
trade leaves and rocks
for lakes or ponds,
returning to his watery roots.

Poetic Form ~ A **Pregunta** (Spanish for "question") is a Spanish poetic form where the first stanza (also called a verse) poses a question and the second answers it.

Ghost Crab

Gliding on four pairs of legs,
she slinks away
from hungry birds,
blending into the sand—
except—SURPRISE!—her two beady eyes.

Do teachers really have eyes in the back of their heads?

Kids might think so. Ghost crabs, on the other hand, don't need eyes there. They can already see 360 degrees at a time. Named for their ghostly pale color, ghost crabs **camouflage** with the sand to avoid predators. If that doesn't work, they can also make a rumbling noise with their stomach to scare off enemies.

Emerald Green Sea Slug

Feasting on algae,
this small, solar-powered slug
slithers through water,
ruffled like a marshy leaf,
part plant and part animal.

Poetic Form ~ A Tanka is a Japanese poetic form that stretches one sentence over five lines in a 5, 7, 5, 7, 7 syllable pattern.

Ever hear that you are what you eat?

These sea slugs get their bright green color from eating algae. The algae contain **chloroplasts** that allow the slugs to draw energy from the sun, a process called photosynthesis. Plants can photosynthesize, but it's rare that animals can, too. This unique ability means they can go a whole year without eating.

Blue-Footed Booby

No candy hearts or rose bouquets,
no string quartets or moonlit gaze.
For ladies seeking true romance,
it's all about his clumsy dance!

Poetic Form ~ A **quatrain** is a four-line poem or a four-line stanza (also called a verse) that is part of a longer poem. The name comes from the French word "quatre" for "four."

Who needs blue suede shoes when you have blue feet?

Not these birds. Male blue-footed boobies strut, stomp, and show off to females. European explorers probably laughed at the birds' blue-footed boogie, so they named them "booby." It's based on the Spanish word "bobo," meaning silly or foolish. For female boobies, there's nothing silly about this **courtship dance**. They think the bluer the feet, the healthier and more attractive the mate!

If you were a snail, how would you hide from birds and fish?

Very carefully! Violet snails use **countershading** to outsmart predators as they float along the ocean's surface. Their coloring is so clever, similar countershading has been used for some military planes: dark on top, light on the bottom.

Violet Snail

I sail upon a sudsy raft,
a work of mollusk handicraft.
My ombré shell's a smart disguise
to help me blend with seas and skies.
When hungry birds fly overhead,
they dine on other foods instead.
As schools of fish lurk underneath …

I drift away from fearsome teeth!

Poetic Form ~ A **persona** is a poem
that uses a speaker or narrator who is
clearly not the poet. In this case, a snail.
It does not have to rhyme.

Does a bright pink manta ray sound fishy to you?

An 11-foot pink manta ray was first spotted in 2015. It was nicknamed Inspector Clouseau after the bumbling detective in the Pink Panther movies. Scientists believe the manta ray's unusual coloring may be caused by a condition called **erythyrism.** It makes skin appear red or pink.

Poetic Form ~ A **concrete** poem takes the physical shape of its subject, like this manta ray.

Pink Manta Ray

In a
sea of teal,
a blink of pink!
Fins flutter, graceful as a ballerina
and strong like a blue whale, somersaulting between
coral reefs. As fish nibble on his skin,
the gentle giant rests.
Once clean, he
darts off
to a
new
a
d
v
e
n
t
u
r
e.

Picasso Bug

Their brushstrokes dazzle …
but it's their horrible smell
you'll remember most.

Poetic Form ~ A **Haiku** is a Japanese poetic form that usually explores nature and includes three lines with a specific syllable pattern: 5, 7, 5.

How do you think this bug got its name?

Picasso bugs (also called Zulu Hud bugs) look like a masterpiece by artist
Pablo Picasso with bright colors and abstract shapes. But beware! These
tiny, oval-shaped insects are related to the stink bug. When disturbed, they
unleash a nasty odor. This is called **chemical defense** and is designed to
ward off predators.

Nature's Masterpiece

Rosy pinks, regal blues, radiant greens
Adorn birds, bugs, snails, slugs.
Instead of paint on canvas,
Nature colors feathers, fur, skin, scales.
But if some see these creatures as
Oddball or off-the-wall,
Why not delight in their whimsy and wonder?

newt

crab

frog

Poetic Form ~ An **acrostic** is a poem where certain letters in each line spell out a word or phrase.

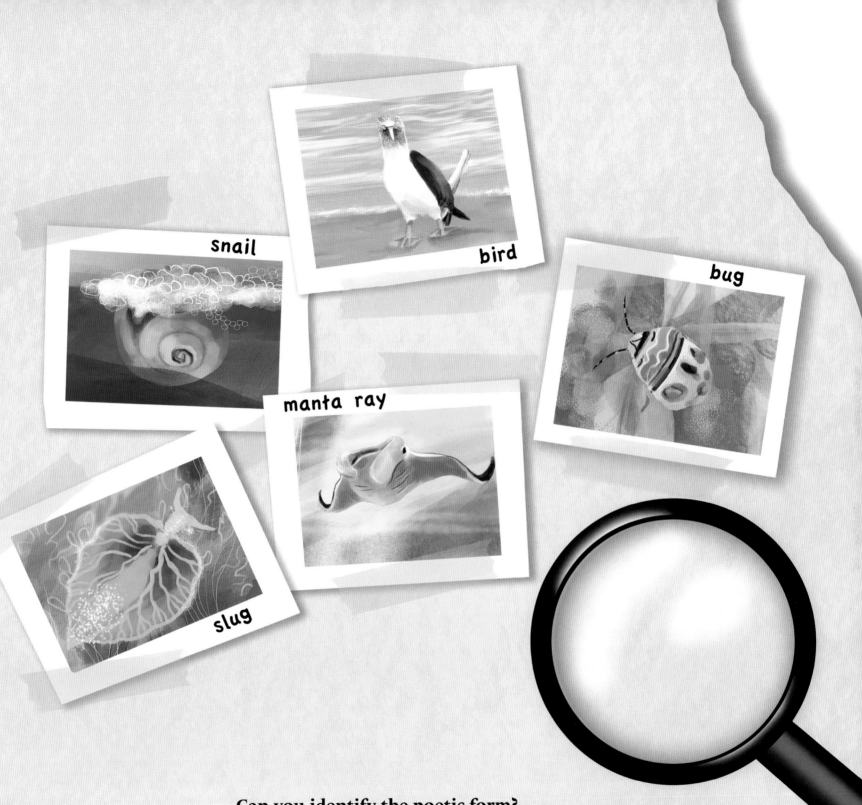

snail

bird

bug

manta ray

slug

Can you identify the poetic form?

This book includes different poetic forms like haiku, tanka, and concrete poems. Can you match the poems on the pages that follow with the correct poetic form presented in the first part of this book? Find the answers in the back!

Red Velvet Ant

Ouch! Beware red velvet ants,
who lurk in woods or fields by night.
Their fuzzy thorax red and black,
their stinger cruel and full of bite.

Does red velvet make you crave dessert?

Don't be fooled by their name! Red velvet ants are not a cake nor are they actually ants. They're wasps that measure up to three-quarters of an inch long. Females only look like ants because they don't have wings. However, they have powerful stingers and are usually **nocturnal**. Males have wings but no stingers.

Green Honeycreeper

Pecking at berries,
her feathers blend into leaves,
dodging deadly snakes.

Ever hear that birds of a feather flock together?

Green honeycreepers are birds of different colors that flock together.
They are **dimorphic**, meaning the males and females don't look
alike. Males have a teal body with a black hood, while females are
the color of green grass.

Soaring and trilling
above canopies of trees,
he spreads turquoise wings.

Banana Slug

I glide along a single foot
Sloooowly leaving trails of slime.
Sensors sniffing, reaching forward,
But wait! A leaf! It's dinnertime.

Do these slugs remind you of anything?

Banana slugs may look like a yellow fruit, but their slime numbs predators' tongues, so they sure don't taste fruity. They are **detritivores**, meaning they help leaves, moss, and other matter decompose.

Lilac-Breasted Roller

In
woodlands
or savannas,
this daredevil dives
and dazzles, flaunting
plumage in lilac and
sapphire blue. Fearless
like a stunt pilot, he shows
off with a "zaaak!" before
joining his mate, their nest
/ / high
/ / in a
X X tree.

Where do you think animals get their names?

Rollers are named for the male's energetic courtship flight, featuring dips, dives, and mid-air rolls as they squawk loudly. Rollers also swoop down from their perches to catch food such as grasshoppers or lizards. Bush fires have devastated many animals, but these birds have made a smart **adaptation:** hunting just outside the fires as their prey escapes.

Glossary of Terms

Adaptation: Behaviors or physical traits that an animal developed to survive.

Aposematic coloration: Noticeable coloring that makes an animal less attractive to potential predators. Also called advertising coloration or warning coloration.

Camouflage: Coloring that blends into its surroundings so the animal can avoid predators.

Chemical defense: Certain plants and animals give off toxins that scare away predators.

Chloroplast: A structure within a plant cell that uses photosynthesis to change sunlight into energy a plant or certain animals can use.

Countershading: A type of camouflage where an animal's coloring is darker on one side and lighter on the other side.

Courtship: The process some animals use for choosing a mate.

Detritivore: Invertebrates that consume decaying plant and animal parts and help it decompose. They are nature's recyclers.

Dimorphic: When males and females of the same species display different physical traits.

Erythyrism: A condition that makes skin appear unusually pink or red. It can be caused by diet or genetics.

Noctural: Describes an animal that is active at night. It's the opposite of diurnal, which describes animals that are active during the day.

Regenerate: When an animal loses a body part and regrows it.

For complimentary educator resource materials and additional source citations, please visit www.gnomeroadpublishing.com.

Selected Sources

"Poison Dart Frogs." National Geographic, 24 Sept. 2018, www.nationalgeographic.com/animals/amphibians/group/poison-dart-frogs/.

"Eastern Newt - Notophthalmus Viridescens." Wildlife Journal Junior, New Hampshire PBS, nhpbs.org/wild/easternnewt.asp.

"Ghost Crab." National Parks Service, U.S. Department of the Interior, www.nps.gov/pais/learn/nature/ghost_crab.htm.

Phone interview with Patrick J. Krug, Professor of Biological Sciences & Graduate Advisor at the California State University – Los Angeles on April 12, 2021.

Blue-Footed Booby. National Geographic, 21 Sept. 2018, www.nationalgeographic.com/animals/birds/b/blue-footed-booby/.

Wu, Katherine J. "Rare Pink Manta Ray Spotted Near Australia's Lady Elliot Island." Smithsonian.com, Smithsonian Institution, 13 Feb. 2020, www.smithsonianmag.com/smart-news/rare-pink-manta-ray-spotted-near-australias-lady-elliot-island-180974196/.

"Velvet Ants." Entomology, University of Kentucky College of Agriculture, Food & Environment, entomology.ca.uky.edu/ef442.

"Green Honeycreeper Female And Male Visit Separately – Feb. 7, 2019." Cornell Lab Birds Cams, 8 Feb. 2019, www.youtube.com/watch?v=-FCyNEbjokw.

Beukes, Lauren. "Interesting Facts on Beautiful Picasso Bugs." Southlands Sun, 2 Aug. 2017, southlandssun.co.za/78541/interesting-facts-beautiful-picasso-bugs.

Crew, Bec. "Violet Snail an Ocean Wanderer." Australian Geographic, 2 Sept. 2018, www.australiangeographic.com.au/blogs/creatura-blog/2014/03/violet-snail-janthina-janthina/.

Petty, Todd. "Photo of the Day: Lilac-Breasted Roller." Audubon, 13 Apr. 2016, www.audubon.org/news/photo-day-lilac-breasted-roller.

"Banana Slug." National Geographic, 20 Dec. 2019, www.nationalgeographic.com/animals/invertebrates/b/banana-slug/.

To Dad for sharing his fascination with the natural world. -SJT

About the Author ~ Susan Johnston Taylor writes for kids and adults. Her magazine articles have appeared in *Dramatics, FACES, Fast Company, Entrepreneur, Scout Life, Highlights for Children*, and many others. A strong believer in the power of poetry, Susan co-teaches a summer poetry camp through Austin Bat Cave, an Austin, Texas-based nonprofit that offers writing programs for kids and teens. In addition to *Animals in Surprising Shades*, she has written several children's books for the educational market. Visit Susan online at www.staylorwrites.com.

About the Illustrator ~ Annie Bakst is an illustrator and designer living in Vermont. The colors and textures of animals and nature have inspired the work in this lovely poetic book. Traditional gouache drawings and paintings were enhanced digitally in the artwork on each page. Annie has illustrated graphic novels, children's books, and murals, and has had several gallery shows. She has won numerous national design awards and a New York City Society of Illustrators Award. For more information about Annie, visit anniebakststudio.com.

Special thanks to artist Bonnie Kelso for cover, end sheet, and book design services.

ANSWER KEY

Red Velvet Ant ~ This is a quatrain poem.
Green Honey Creeper ~ This is a haiku poem.
Banana Slug ~ This is a persona poem.
Lilac-Breasted Roller ~ This is a concrete poem.

Now pick an animal you like and write a poem of your own!